CLEVELAND STATE UNIVERSITY POETRY CENTER
NEW POETRY

Michael Dumanis, Series Editor

Samuel Amadon, *The Hartford Book*
John Bradley, *You Don't Know What You Don't Know*
Lily Brown, *Rust or Go Missing*
Elyse Fenton, *Clamor*
Emily Kendal Frey, *The Grief Performance*
Dora Malech, *Say So*
Shane McCrae, *Mule*
Helena Mesa, *Horse Dance Underwater*
Philip Metres, *To See the Earth*
Zach Savich, *The Firestorm*
Sandra Simonds, *Mother Was a Tragic Girl*
S. E. Smith, *I Live in a Hut*
Mathias Svalina, *Destruction Myth*
Allison Titus, *Sum of Every Lost Ship*
Liz Waldner, *Trust*
Allison Benis White, *Self-Portrait with Crayon*
Jon Woodward, *Uncanny Valley*

For a complete listing of titles please visit
www.csuohio.edu/poetrycenter

RENDER

✿

AN APOCALYPSE

isbn 978-0-9860257-3-0
First edition
5 4
This book is published by the Cleveland State
University Poetry Center,2121 Euclid Avenue, Cleveland,
Ohio 44115-2214 www.csuohio.edu/poetrycenter and is
distributed bySPD / Small Press Distribution, Inc.
www.spdbooks.org.
Cover image: 2012, illustration © Arwen Donahue
Render / An Apocalypse was designed and typeset by
Ryan Kelly in Chapparal.

Library of Congress Cataloging-in-Publication Data

Howell, Rebecca Gayle.
[Poems. Selections]
Render : an Apocalypse / Rebecca Gayle Howell. —First
edition pages cm
Includes bibliographical references and index.
"Distributed by SPD / Small Press Distribution, Inc."
—T.p. verso Poems.
Winner of the 2012 Cleveland State University Poetry
Center First Book Prize.
ISBN 978-0-9860257-3-0 (paperback : acid-free paper)
I. Title.
PS3608.O95525R46 2013
811'.6--dc23

2013000070

RENDER

❊

AN APOCALYPSE

❊ ❊

REBECCA GAYLE HOWELL

❊ ❊ ❊

CLEVELAND STATE UNIVERSITY
POETRY CENTER
CLEVELAND, OHIO

The Petition

✿

Foreword

Render / An Apocalypse is a book about need,
about what we must do, or have others do for
us, to fulfill that need, be it hunger or desire or
connection with something larger, something
outside ourselves, outside the little cage of our
need. In living with these poems for a few months
now I have occasionally tried to imagine what
image will be chosen for the cover of this book. I
sense it will be a black and white photograph—A
bare tree in a barren field? No, that wouldn't be
right, for the energy of these poems is perhaps
the opposite of barren, though perhaps you too
will feel a cold wind as you turn each page. Nor
do I know how this book has come (dear reader)
to be in your hands, though I sense you will need
to live with these poems for awhile, to let their
power seep into you.

A fervor runs through each page, which when I first
encountered it struck me as nearly religious (in
the best sense of the word), yet upon subsequent
readings seems to settle into the demotic, the
messy stuff of our everyday. The voice is strong, it
insists, it compels, it occasionally lunges, though
it can also lull, for very simply there is work to be
done.

On the surface this is a series of how-to poems,
yet these poems, when the apocalypse comes, may
actually save you, when you too find yourself
stranded, hungry, and friendless. Or maybe the
apocalypse has already come (how would we know?),
and these poems are the hopeful by-products
of the aftermath. As might be expected, in this
(perhaps) unfamiliar world "there are rules," as
well as flashes of beauty (this perfume / of ruin

they are made for"), but there is no winking, no ironic comfort, no safety in the sense that we are (or will be allowed to be) mere tourists to this world—After all, the sun is always going down, we need to eat. I am reminded of something Whitman once said, whereby he connects Socrates to Barthe:

> The process of reading is not a half-sleep, but, in the highest sense, an exercise, a gymnast's struggle; that the reader is to do something for himself, must be on the alert, must himself or herself construct indeed the poem, argument, history, metaphysical essay—The text furnishing the hints, the clue, the start or frame-work. Not the book needs so much to be the complete thing, but the reader of the book does.

To enter into these poems one must be fully committed, as the poet is, to seeing this world as it is, to staying with it, moment by moment, day by day. Yet these poems hold a dark promise: this is how you can do it, but you must be fully engaged, which means you must be fully awake, you must wake up inside it. As we proceed, the how-to of the beginning poems subtly transforms, as the animals (or, more specifically, *the livestock*) we are engaging begin to, more and more, become part of us, literally and figuratively—We enter inside of that which we devour.

> Then step inside her
>
> your arms inside her
> death like it is a room

> your private room
> peculiar and clean

This is from the poem "How To Kill a Hog," which ends with the line "do not turn away," a line which contains the energy of the whole—terse, distilled, rendered—do not turn away from anything.

—Nick Flynn
November 2012
Brooklyn, NY

For Dulcena and Johnny Neace. And for my mother.

"Without tenderness, we are in hell."

—Adrienne Rich

✲

Do you not work? Does your sweat not fall
like bread from the firmament of your brow
your thirst and hunger mounting, your stomach
gorged—Your coulter your hand winding
worm roads into soil, have you not been cursed?
Brother who is not the keeping brother, tiller
of earth—Are you not a mouth that eats
the mites of day called dust (that filth wind
to which you will return) and do you not
call it banquet *(styrofoam angels all around)*
do you not call it feast? *You want You want*
what you want You cannot help that anyhow   now

1 How to Wake

Learn your lesson
from the calf

Look how he rams his head
into the cow's sack

when she does not drop
when she holds her drink

like a warm secret
Let her know your thirst is there

a wide-mouthed bucket
on the ground

If you want first milk
first light sweet cream

first chore done
be mean

Shout her name
Force her leg back

Her tail swatting you
Your fist pounding her

Your face strained against
the spate of flies

her hot dirt body
horns rising open bone

eroded by air and age
Do not be ashamed

of this your private
pleasure

Take charge
Tell her your secrets

Your lips low against her udder
like you are dream-twitching

and who is there
to see you No one No one

Watch yourself
You'll get shit on

or kicked in the head

2 How to Kill a Rooster

Because he's spurred you
grab him by his neck and his legs

Hold him in both your hands
Look him in the eye

Let him ask
if you are to kill him today

then tell him yes   say *yes*
with your own eye

just before you take him
to the clothes line

and tie him up
by his yellow feet

Take a blade
Cut his throat

Watch his blood drip
to the ground

Watch his wings spread
and flap and flap and

while you watch this desperate bird
and think to yourself

I will never be like him

remember in the end you will
drop him in boiling water

pluck each of his oily feathers
between your fingers

Remember in the end
you will taste him

for good

3 How to Kill a Hen

Enter the night coop
whistling

Through your teeth
sing

In this awful world of sorrow
sing

In this wicked path of sin

Tuck her
under your arm

and walk away
from the laying birds

the cuckold-morning
rising in their dumb wings

Walk away from sleep

Make sure her hollow bones
alone will be warmed by it

your wordless bellows
breast

For this is your gift to her

Tell her
you never think of tomorrow

Tell her
what you'd lose in the end

Enter the night coop
whistling

Leave whistling
Climb the dust hill

When you get up
to the house

ring once the orbit
of your failing

Over your head
a breaking neck

For this is your gift to her:

You can hear your savior calling
barefaced and feather red

4 How to Build a Root Cellar

Let the bounty rot
Let the day's gas drift up

through the floorboards
Let your stomach bleed

Work
as if your shovel

strikes only rock
As if the soil under

the soil was sold
while you slept

When we birth
we bury the placenta

twice as deep
as we do the body

where its smell cannot draw
predators And you are

the predator
And you are the prey

This is the paper you can't place
The scrap signed *Deed*

Most mammals most mothers
eat the after

We bury it
eat the before—

To build a root cellar

borrow cold from the ground
Dark from the night

Dig into the hill
Dig on the hill's north side

Call your own name until
you have one

You have one
You have one

5 A Catalog of What You Have

The offal

the slop, swill—pitiless
river—the beak the bone

newspaper pink
with sinew's oil

piled up on the kitchen floor
cumulous and close

the air of drippings
the wet air of fat

How when the animal opens
the naming begins

kept   not kept

and how when the animal empties
a sugar sets in

a pressure barometric
and all that's left will be rendered by it

made small and smaller by it
until what is there to name

but the lye and the burning clean

6 A Catalog of What You Do Not Have

Enough

7 How to Preserve

Boil the water bath
Drop glass

Drop hands
finger tips

speaking mouth
tongue

Drop memory
like glass

down into the bath
Bring up the heat

slow so none notice
nothing shatters

so the tongue can think
it might not be burned

might go on telling
what does not want to be told

This is how you preserve

Sterilize
Scald

before packing the jars
with glory

O Harvest
Hard won

and terrible

8 A Brief Atlas for Leave-taking

The tree of knowledge
of touch and age

grows in the perfect orchard
of your lungs

And loneliness
like black snakes dropping

like roads
dropping from every limb

9 A Brief Atlas for Return

When the herd arrives
you will be lost

in the field without
the cover of trees

your days wet and natal
with wide heat

your sense absent
your drought throat—

Behold their approach
silence of their silence

how they rend the soil
with their hooves

smelling blood-
guilt seeped underneath

how they will not
leave what was abandoned

how they circle you
mother tongues

upon your forehead
your neck

your back and bold chest
anointing you

new and without scent
without name

10 How to Plant by the Signs

When the ground is lit
when your back, hands, intent are lit

full well
full dawn of dark

when the tide swells
(forget sea)

when the tide swells in soil unseen
root stem leaf

when the moon is in its age

plant that which rises
above the ground to bloom

full well
full fruit

in the old of the moon
When the sign is in the loins or breast

when the sign is in your feet
calloused (yes bare)

if what you wish is to harvest
if what you wish is to reap

grow the hour long

take the seed of secret
in your palm

spread it like a witness
spread it like a disease

11 How to Be Civilized

Because she once ran forest and field
but came to you when called—loyal beast—

because her hooves are formed
for soil fallen leaves long rains

for earth that gives way
beneath foot and weight and foraging

because she did come
but might go astray

we now keep the pen
keep control

Build it tall with walls
Build it deep

with indoor outdoor
space

Make the pig think
she has a choice

she can defecate
away from her feed

she can still be clean
Build a wood floor angled high

so you can wash out her shit and piss
if you have the time

so you can come to her
and take each leg up each hoof

and scrub or else she'll swell

her feet sore from splinters
and inert days

She'll just
lie down

her muscles atrophied
her meat in ruin

You will have to quit
whatever it is you are doing

and take a stick
and prod her

take your boot
and kick her

get up get up
If you have the time

build a pen tall with walls
She will adapt

This is how we are civilized

12 How to Wean a Hog

Bait her
from the warm teat

with cereal
powdered milk

sugar

After that she will eat
your waste

Raise the animal
to trust you

and it won't matter
what you bring her

She will scuttle to the fence
snorting steam

when she hears you beating
the slop bucket drum

when she doesn't see you coming
with her human eyes

13 How to Build Trust

See how she rakes against
the fence the other pigs her straw

how she's tried, she really has
and what a simple thing

for you to stop
stacking hay

hosing away her filth
stop, what, maybe to smoke

your hands already out of your pockets
your teeth already clenched

what a simple thing
her head wrenching toward light

your fingers thick with her wire
hair as you think about

the work ahead
its musk and hazard

how this is not about love

as she comes to you
her whole muzzle

inside your coat
her breath

probing your chest
how she roots you

the yellow sky smoldering
how she asks for more

14 How to Be a Man

Don't miss
Shoot her square

If you squeal her
you can't shoot again

There are rules

You'll be made
to chase her

and she will run
in black-dawn air

cold and clean
And you will run

And you will hear her
screaming

the other hogs
screaming

the other men
jeering at you, less than them

And you'll be made to catch her
but you won't

And you'll be made to take her
four hundred six hundred

pound body to the ground
pin her

bleed her
throat   But you won't

The black-dawn air
cold and mean

The wet fog your breath
Or is it hers

15 How to Be a Pig

Be clever
Be quick to learn

Dream in color
Dream in techni-

color trees
Sleep forage

between gold leaves
Squeeze out

twenty young a year
Make them fight

for your teats
Dream that one

is flame tip
black spots

Dream that he
gets the teat he wants

See red
while you

let the flies
land

Throw
tantrums

Stop throw-
ing tantrums

Pavlov says

All pigs are hysterical
All pigs are hysterical

Pavlov says

Desire:

She must be without it

If she is in heat
if when you put your hands

on either side of her hog back
and press down as to open her

if she stands still
and ready

her meat will taste
strong like a boar's

You want to lie
back wait

quiet

until she does not know
what she wants more

Size:

If you come out back to find
she fills and cannot rotate in her pen

if she is more than twice your weight
you're late

You want to overfeed her but not
overfeed her

You want to make sure
for your sake

she is well kept   bloated
but not threatening

that on her day of reckoning
she feels the stretch of her skin

and knows she did not choose
her body   hot and exhausting

knows that you chose for her
every day of her eating even this one

knows she needs you
to call her *sooey sooey*

and she will show you how she comes

Sex:

If you risk a male to slaughter
plan ahead

When he is still a piglet
grip him between your thighs

Take his hind legs push them

back like a woman's legs

when she wants you
while the cut is prepared

Keep his head down
Once the scrotum opens

the testicles should pop
Cut both off

Throw them in the weeds
Coat his wound with ashes

while your legs now soaked, burning
stand

Weather:

The air must be so cold
as to stun the flies

for as long as possible
against this perfume

of ruin they are made for
every winged beat of waiting

so cold it stuns you when you walk out
in that noiseless hour before

your dawn your lungs
to seize as they wake

into this embrace
your mind to seize

when you first inhale
the gun's sharp glare

On that day your day of killing
let nothing freeze

You must in this winter of your weighing choice
be a man

Act
Act like you know what you know

17 How to Be an Animal

Forget you are an animal

Forget ancient rummaging
pigs wild in their snouts

Forget you ran with them

Wild among trees
Wild in your cheer

18 How to Cook the Lungs

They cannot be kept
Feed them to your children

Feed them to the dog
Boil them with the heart

which no one eats alone
Boil them with the backbone

Who knows how breath of god
cooks down to mash

Days of work
of cold blight air

its viral flame
of inhale exhale

waste

Gone   Gone
They cannot be kept

Feed me to your children
Feed me to the dog

the raccoon the fox
the rat

the foraging mouths
the shameless ones

19 How to Cook the Head

Hand it over to someone else:

Let him cut my ears off
My tongue, out

Set them to soak
Even my snout will be split

even my eyes must go
You understand why

My blood must be let
Your loneliness

Your silenced desire with it
He'll quarter me

Halve me
You understand why

This new stew requires
simple parts:

Bay leaves
One load onions

Five pounds salt
Your will

Fill the kitchen with your smell

20 How to Cook the Brain

Go mad in pens

You who once had taste for roots grasses fruits
flowers
now lose all sense

Eat carcass Eat insects worms   tree bark
Eat garbage Eat even other pigs

You who once ate light

eat night
eat coal

Let the hard black rock of want
tear the skin of your prized intestines

Squeal Squeal for more

21 How to Kill a Hog

Do you remember how close
you were to her

when she was farrowing
and she needed you

her bawling drawing
you out of bed

a bad dream
how you washed her vulva, soft

warm water over your own
hands how you scrubbed

even your fingernails
under your fingernails

before you came to the pen and the sun-
flower oil you coated yourself in

so she would not chafe
even as she hemorrhaged

and how against all this
bloody shit and hay

you took each piglet
out of her night and into yours

into your palm and cleared
its mouth its nose of mucus

how you brought breath
to each set of tiny lungs

how you washed
how you opened her

That is how to touch her now

Once she is hung
and cut straight cut

from rectum to neck
while the other men

take their cigarettes
find quick coffee, food

Lag behind wait
until the barn is empty

until you are alone
Then step inside her

your arms inside her
death like it is a room

your private room
peculiar and clean

Gather her organs up
into your arms

like you once did your mother's robes
when you were a boy who knew nothing

but the scent of sweat and silk
Hold her and inhale

Before reaching all the way around
to snip the last tendon

before you cut the stomach
intestines kidney liver

before you cut her heart
out

and she drops into you
and drops down

into the cold wash tub
of this day

close your eyes just once
just once

do not turn away

Because the fly
does not rest

because it is a machine
its body formed from bronze

its head, bullion
its wings from glass

because this small alloy
cast in flight

needs muscle
still humid with life

you have no time
to lose

After the slaughter
after the neighbors have gone

and the blood has soaked the ground
after the knife

drop your cracked hands
into the ice bath

Knead her shoulders, thighs
knead each length

slow like it is your own
sore from this day's already long work

Rub her with salt black pepper
molasses and fear

Keep that glowing scavenger
away from what it needs

because you are a machine
and this is what you are here for

When the peach trees blossom
when your weather has turned

lay hickory and apple
lay sassafras, fuel

fresh split tender and green
In this open house

logs transcendent with air
no mud or mortar or screen

start the smoke rolling
uncontrollable

great smothering
great next coming

Each blazing day counted
by every pound of flesh

you own

Machine not machine The aluminum shine
        of self—Breath the key-wound spring
Breath its leap release What more than automata
        Than the pull of bronze wire
rigging the saw blade rigging the bellows
        the valve the spiral cog that moves
the leg's knee to step or the mouth's wood jaw
        to drop and sing Machine not machine
the same pulse A talking radio a bald light bulb
        lure dangling an electric cookstove
The kitchen wallpaper a trellis of roses
        in perfect grids like cities The clock's deaf
gears teethed and turning This is your hour
        These are the beasts of the field
and you have called them

Call to tomorrow like you would a cow
      and like a cow it will not come
when called (stubborn girl) rain herd lining
      the sycamore's shadow her black
body thick with refusal hard and fast
      Do not resent her for her rest
Just outside your window as you wash dishes
      as you skin dirt potatoes
Yes tomorrow comes on its own
      The engine a combustion internal
of piston-mind, intake compression and you
      are exhausted wet mouths
flies and the muck of roots shoved under
      your scrubbing nails What contraption
is there—What is built or born that hears you?
      Your whisper peels in spiral carousels
Your splintered table Your bone and wire hands
      The thin knife twists
Heat drips from the roof The afternoon storms
      You are in Think to get out
Yield unceasing End without end Harvest
      Then a darkness sets
one orange lamp to see by
      Why not give up—Why not fall
to your knees as all knees fall?
      Things being   as they are

As they are—In this house
        with windows in this house with doors
you come to the counter
        you come to the linoleum killing floor
Carrying a female made to roost, a womb
        Your womb before yolk and time took the shell
You are not a machine
        Though on days like this—
Take the hen, your automated fingers
        sliding over her membrane milk-glass skin
tired tough white-plucked dead
        Ready the grounded bird hollow bones wasted
Ready the fat bird
        Pull her legs apart, clavicular, pull her wings
For you stand without wings
        For you stand at the sink with exile in your mouth
and you crave it like salt
        that carcass so warmed as to hatch the viral strain
Lift her soaked in the sewage of hours and cellophane
        Lift her from the tray
Say grace to the drain to the lard Fry Watch her marrow
        once red with ruined flight   brown
Then from the skillet suck and sip the oil
        anointed with standing still: an honest tonic
for your condition—
        The absence that you will

But what if your absence
        were like the absence of gnats?
The scattershot flight of one who does not
        have life enough to leave
one who stirs the air in minute-winds
        then takes a lonesome going
behind the spigot or hog's ear or worse
        where no one sees (unless they see
to be relieved) Your absence a fluster a waste
        Today you've cooked a bird
That's something You've made food of death
        Look at me says the bird without a neck
Look at me now A bug arguing with a chicken
        Save the looking for the mean sun
Save the carcass for stock
        Tonight you will dream
a mockingbird, brass bugle for a beak
        Its tree grows out from your head
leaves of seeing glass   darkly
        a tap from which mercury draws
silver and hot   Mercy or not
        These are the blazing days
and you are asked to love

✿   *and you are asked to love*

To want is not to love
        That raccoon scratching at the porch door
tail of lock washer rings, grease-hair
        He wants He takes whatever he can
into his hands up to his mouth He learns by taking
        as you once learned by tongue
Your house his crop of new fruit
        Your idle hour his equinox
Not every creature learns this way
        You have to be a blood and guts bulldozer
a drone scrounge You have to not care
        how you get what you get But you are
the complicated animal hairless and shining
        You are the one with reasons—
Break the jars on the cellar floor
        Sauerkraut, beets   you'll be ankle deep
in soil come glass and cannot move
        to leave   or else go home

Since there's nothing else to kill
        take the slate rock piled out back
and target blue jays as they hawk
        grasshoppers on the dirt road
Since there is nothing else to drink
        take the beans from the stove
spoon off some soup pour it down your baby's throat
        Your milk cake dry your mouth of poke
Since this fencerow is no longer your fencerow
        since you scorned this fertile ground
your homeplace now   a mark of what you do not own
        Pull up a post, store in its pit
your neighbor's bread pinched from her one plate
        Risk the worm and weevil
even as her eyes fall in like sinkholes
        where sumac and tires where engines
return to the dissolving earth—
        Even as her dump-eyes cave
Isn't this the way?
        To think the blue jay's song will lift
from the river of your tongue because you
        swallowed its lungs Forget singing birds
Drive north Find an infinite field
        Drive until you hear the word *Repent*
in your ears—That great horned owl
        that raptor that hoot The sky like the arms
of a spreader coming down then the road sign:
        Hell is Real Recite it: *Hell is Real*
As you have been stolen from, steal

✻   *As you have been stolen from, steal*

As you have starved, say *No one will starve*
        The chicken's blood stains everyone's hands
Everyone's hands, stained   (and so cleansed)
        Walk off Or don't
Tomorrow comes on its own
        Call instead to your regrets
your chiggers your ticks Each nail-head body
        crawling you, your length a blade of grass
Watch how it labors to bury its biting head
        to find the wet night it knows is there
This is your inheritance:
        to be the singing blood meal, unaware

                    —Touch!
                        That nimbus That choice

Acknowledgments

I am grateful to the editors of the following publications in which these poems first appeared, sometimes in earlier forms: *32 Poems*: "How to Wean a Hog." *Barely South:* "How to Be a Man," "How to Kill a Hog." *Ecotone:* "How to Kill a Rooster." *Great River Review:* "A Calendar of Blazing Days." *Indiana Review:* "How to Be a Pig." *The Louisville Review:* "A Brief Atlas for Leave-taking," "A Brief Atlas for Return." *Lumberyard:* "How to Wake," "The Petition." *Naugatuck River Review:* "How to Dig a Root Cellar." *Ninth Letter:* "How to Build Trust." *Still: The Journal:* "How to Kill a Hen," "How to Preserve," "How to Be Civilized." *Southern Indiana Review:* "How to Time the Kill." *storySouth:* "A Catalog of What You Have," "How to Cure." *Wind: A Journal of Writing & Community:* "How to Plant by the Signs." *Yew:* "How to Cook the Lungs," "How to Cook the Head," "How to Cook the Brain." "How to Be an Animal" was included in *Bigger Than They Appear: An Anthology of Very Short Poems* (Accents Publishing, 2011).

I would also like to thank the following for their support: the Cleveland State University Poetry Center, the Fine Arts Work Center, the PhD creative writing faculty at Texas Tech University, the MFA faculty at Drew University, the Kentucky Foundation for Women, and the North Lexington Guild of Art & Philosophy.

Especially: Landon Antonetti, Vicki Bee, Arwen Donahue, Kathy Doyle, Michael Dumanis, Vaughan Fielder, Boris Fishman, Nick Flynn, Carolyn Forché, Frank Giampietro, Darla Himeles, Ryan Kelly, Andrew Meredith, Mihaela Moscaliuc, Alicia Ostriker, Nancy Pearson, Betsy Reese, Salvatore Scibona, Roger Skillings, Erik Tuttle, Michael Waters, Ellen Doré Watson, David Wagoner, Phoebe Wagoner, Marcus Wicker, Crystal Wilkinson, Elizabeth Winston

And Wendell Berry.

Rebecca Gayle Howell is the translator of Amal al-Jubouri's *Hagar Before the Occupation/Hagar After the Occupation* (Alice James Books, 2011). Among her awards are two fellowships from the Fine Arts Work Center and a Pushcart Prize. Native to Kentucky, Howell is the Poetry Editor at *Oxford American*.